T0166779

Tyres and Driveways

RICHARD KEMP

Tyres and Driveways

CAT'S EYE
EYEWEAR PAMPHLET SERIES 2020

First published in 2020
by Black Spring Press Group
Suite 333, 19-21 Crawford Street
Marylebone, London W1H 1PJ
United Kingdom

Typeset with graphic design by Edwin Smet

All rights reserved © 2020 Richard Kemp

The right of Richard Kemp to be identified as authors of this work has been asserted in

accordance with section 77 of the Copyright, Designs and Patents Act 1988

ISBN 978-1913606-76-3

WWW.EYEWEARPUBLISHING.COM

This pamphlet is dedicated to Richard Nieper

Table of contents

I

II

I

The Sea Speaks Lion

This won't go to sleep night,
this quiet in the shadow of the grasses night,
this going to be a breeze turning the sails of the crazy golf night.
The Coke can is a small cave.
It never gets dark on the beach.
The irrigation channels that run back, the night is laying down in them,

the night is laying down in them to be the whole world asleep.
The rusty fence and thorns and fox-prints falling through
their own blue light. The sea clattering and crashing and green losing itself
and finding no memory,
building walls and smashing walls
all night down East Parade; the sea's broken wings and refrigerators

and blood and carved toads' bellies and young fathers and cloaks,
the sea's bells and crickets,
rag-flowers, watch boxes, and the divan bed,
prams, tendrils, and restless summits
and folding black doves, overlain destroyed shoes,
roosters, horse skeletons, whistle blasts and fog,

this won't go to sleep night,
this quiet in the bushes night.

The Start of Sylvia

Sylvia had a red mouth from Cherryade;
she held a dead mouse, crisp and grey,
the size of an old fifty pence.

Walking in the pitchy night in her dad's mac
that smelt like the flags in the town's museum,
her two doll hands ripped out the grape stomach
of the mouse,
the blood, signal to her laughter.

Back in the hall we danced like scalded moths,
our thin bodies spun or stood,
a group of boys and a group of girls,
with the band of fathers playing music unknown to us.

Lena in the Odeon, Clacton-on-Sea

Jay can say Lena squeezed his arm when that bloke
gets garroted in *The Godfather*.
Jay can say Lena did turn up,
didn't say much but let him buy her a 7Up.
Jay can say the back of Lena's neck
has the thinnest blonde hair.
He can say Lena's ankle has a transfer tattoo of a Care Bear
that won't come off.
Jay can say Lena's shoulders are white like a starving greyhound.
Jay can say the flecks of green in Lena's eyes are like seaweed.
Jay has that for Jay.

August was an Empty Coke Can

What dramas my cousin had with her hair,
summer of the non-conformists,
trains standing and the violet nowhere that sleeps on the beach,
summer of balloons caught in the high roof of the pier's arcade,
9-carat gold chains bought by brothers for girls to let the brothers
stare at textured ceilings and feel like empty stadia,

summer of sun that was a lion running up a mountain,
cupboards of ants eating Ryvita, past midnight's cinema walls echoing
the sea's iron door banging all night,
of 10p horror chambers, tin horse rifle range near desertion,
bowling alley ceiling wheel track throb,

drinking in the car parks of Saturday,
sand and Coke and ashtrays,
muffled freedom look-out points, and the revering way
men peer into the engines of cars.

He Had Been Walking Where Things Were Yet to be Built

and there were piles of sand and driveways with no houses,
young trees, For Sale signs and morning-warmed tarmac,
pink-blue sky, corn in ditches at the side of the road.

Water was trapped in the tunnels of builders' yellow plastic pipes.
Grass was growing through the gravel
of the new community hall.

*

Uncle, you're without enemies now,
the horizon is sleepy with nightingales,
the electric's un-metered and your shoes now fit you.

They have taken your chair and shot it to pieces with rifles.
You have stopped-up your youth it's true,
but this time your trees are memories that lived.

Foxes are in the hill that they will never abandon,
and my nan, your mother, is delighted with your strong arms,
and your dog does not bark at anyone.

II

Pier, Maybe Sun, Maybe Breeze

A man, legs out, hot day, the brakes of some machine and
amplifier, the remnants of everything spectral, a huge model

of an Indian Chief guarding the milling crescent shoulders,
July a tricky integer of falling, rescuing a kind of giving themselves

up, mirror maze, the put away gifts of the main arena, the pockets
emptied of scars, their slowly turning baby carriage, plates aligned

on tables, the light, the main road, the bench by the main road,
the way we see personalised T-Shirts personalised,

gun sights aligned for Pomagne, bear, or echo in the mountain of
damp nothing of the roof, the pall of arch night complaints,

distended heaped runways of coins, weak crane grabs, nonchalant
walk to signage and the glazed cheeks of sixth formers out-staring

parents that weren't enough, when the eyes flash shoot,
the road's dust is whatever dark suffered and was repeated, the

violence was blessed, the shouts initiations, no one would give up,
we followed the stone road of our hearts, we made our happiness

a fight with every stone, this is a bargain I'm talking about here,
any card you hit means a prize, any card I'm saying,

you choose the prize.

Wile E. Cayote's Dream in the Desert

Her legs spin like roulette wheels at Thanksgiving,
how many times will I whistle and descend to a dot and a cloud?

The precipice – I should have learnt by now,
the cannon's mouth why do I always climb into,

how many giant springs sped me to the void?
Anvils left me flat-headed concertinaed and waddling away

a wheezy valve playing comic songs, how many catapults snapped
or Acme dynamite exploded in the wrong place?

I stretch my arms to the desert,
I saw this night was green and the whites of my eyes were yellow,

I know what dust leaves behind and it's me,
time is ditches I have to run across,

only my breath's sleeping around me and the stars,
I have to marry the desert.

I want a mirrored coffin to know I'm dead or nuclear skates,
though I wouldn't be happy if I wasn't this worn skin,

my arms stretch as wide as the desert.

Sand moving in off the Atlantic, the highway a 40-foot gherkin,
sometimes yesterday is a mountain that gathers up like a clown's trousers,

I'll saw my tongue off, at the end of summer my ribcage is an empty house
and a campfire.

CAT'S EYE

I'm a closing ghost train kids begging their parents for another ride,
but the kids walking away forlorn.

I no longer dream of Indy 500 cars and landing nets,
but darkness and flashlights and border patrols.

I stretch my arms as wide as the desert.

I'm laying on the ground. I'm listening to weeds,
I need lightning so I can shout to the desert 'These trees have

caught fire!' I can put my arms out and touch the sky
and shout again 'THESE TREES HAVE CAUGHT FIRE!'

Town

for Roddy Lumsden

Avalanche of quiet on Carnarvon Road,
tinsel on the floor of the Salvation Army hall,

showroom of Alan Reed Cars, the Texaco sign, like our
uncouth ancestry, gone, the oceans hard to find but you're staring at it.

What were we doing around the dinner table? Our Polaroid flash
eight frosted windows in July, the hot breath of the man selling

photographs, the calm eyes of the woman in the launderette,
the tunnel that becomes a person, mercury scales and blood

of the market, Odeon posters, the air turns cooler,
lawns empty of dress hems, nights of static or put it another way

locusts at the side of the road,
men walking pavements not being a lion or a civilisation

but uncarried-out love behaviours, steep embankments, white hotels.
The weather broke on the steel slide of the crazy golf,

the whale's mouth backdrop to Popeye who doesn't look right.
And the newsagent wants to be the convention that's leaving.

Great xylophone of poverty and the racetrack
views lanes stretching to rooms of men's loud shirts,

rifle ranges of boys shooting targets of bottles and sofas.
Thus we lived and our mouths were open and rain fell into our mouths

so surly and alone as cymbals and reflections and grass,
loosestrife and mint.

Sylvester's Ode to Tweety Pie / Tweety Pie's Break-Up Poem

I

You think I want to eat you but who has not
wanted to consume the beloved,

you, trapezing in the sun
at dusk regard me with a dull and cynical eye

shy figure of a bride drawn-up barred,
sex hidden in a prim spectre evening shines through,

you are burying me under peanut shells,
I circle the house skidding on my tears

all my life, loneliness like an ungripped balloon,
hold me while I breathe on you like a mirror,

me the tired shape that haunts Sunday,
take the sun of my life, my mouth is open.

II

So being alone after that it wasn't like a TV without the remote
or the other way around, or silence without a world,

I try holding a thing and not loving it like you hold a crab,
though now I see a cat's face in bath foam and the grain pile

I say to *myself* make the tea or something,
invent a story about a wasteland and a room that extends

to mountains and mazes and other creatures shouting in rooms.
The fly in this cage, I extend to the darling thing a wing,

reminiscences, these in turn morph into stories about 'what he
really wanted' and how this then turned into a series of weapons

with the look of the sun cutting everything in shadow
half a trapeze, half a mirror, half the water dish

and my legs in shadow and my top half a too-bright yellow eyelash.

Crowds, Amusements, Pens

for Tom Raworth

Pens in display carousels: twenty Edward's, Gary's, Sue's, but no Lena,
the streets continue to the pier

not the approach to Thebes but a kind of wilderness,
kitchens and a trembling child passed Wilkinson's, further than

the knuckles of angry, loud and alone men, their words a stumbling
weight another thing no one can have,

precinct outstretched, cars leaving – fierce untiring, the barber's floor,
the chairs, the men in the chairs,

display of wedding rings, men resurfacing the road, Sew-You Alterations,
Saturday passes bound for Eskimo mountain,

they have dreamt wintry sunlight into the street,
the fire in the throat of the summer we burnt everything

so it could be a mountain, cars coursing everywhere in people
and in me, collar bones and freckles and warm air,

suddenly a deep pool,
the smell of marzipan cooling in a wicker tray,

if you could perform your life in silence it would be a big help
to the rest of us,

lost and outstretched daylight hours explode
walk beside too many unfamiliar streets

The Day, The Discount

A creaky lift is a recipe for ghosts.
The neighbour hasn't drunk enough to be heartfelt.
Of course this place takes cards, it's forgetting we don't do.
The terrifying and beautiful organisers of the ice cream event were coy.
Which way the day goes depends on the shadows.
The rock shop with the dinosaur is closed.
There are men in charcoal suits with unread newspapers sleeping on
        grass inclines.
The sky is colouring the day, stories and quiet people at home in what passes.
The Antiques Centre has sand from Dracula's castle.
A parakeet cage with all the kit.
The owner of the beauty salon keeps the lights on all night.

Pioneer to the Falls

What would it profit to go searching for something
when we could wait right here?

Hoardings billowed in the breeze,
people drinking Coke, trying to remember TV themes,

the poster of Cain and Abel in the classroom something
designed to make you feel bad,

kids grew old chewing wine gums,
the warning had nothing else just its own diamond shape,

the orangey light of evening and tone of people's voices
were part of anyone's tears that fall out of their face

hitting on the floor like gumballs,
some were sleepy or desperately homesick,

old men were speaking about conspiracy and saying *look what
you've done to the tablecloth – yuck!*

This was the perfect part of town to be really indignant,
the scaffolding on the new precinct was like they were building

the Alps, there is a threshold, you are up against it,
someone is saying *what kind of a date is this?*

Marine Parade East

the sojourns of the lonely police
do not make silence something to be proud of,

the consolation of showtunes and the major and dangerous roads,
the sea's rocky pinnacles, tides under flag poles and public squares,

the places of instruction, towers with insignia of swans and tapering
branches, were we supposed to transform all this into love?

Afternoons filled with embarrassment and a kind of anger,
strangers sitting around occupied with kitchen plans –

the middle of a desert and a startled dream.
They say what you are looking for is already here but they're wrong.

Take a look at your situation, these insouciant terms,
the picture in the pool of the first Britons,

a weird and frail absence in the face, arcades, talking
out of a glass case of plush M & Ms,

the sea sleeping, its white dresses thrown off and thrown off.

Discursive

Sun on the names of cars,
bar walls with the dead stars of *Variety*,

mirror frames snowy paths, plaster busts of Mary,
Rodin's *Hands in Prayer*, everything to a white centre,

descent of car park escalators, spectral broadcasts,
slippery waves, wilderness narrowing,

dryers broken, laundry hanging in the street,
Pound Store plates at the front to say to the sky: our dreams.

Just as a clown knows when to fall out of a car
a man shouts 'REPENT!' Phantoms reborn every minute,

the mechanic gets no pleasure from watching television anymore.
Car bonnets struck by a sun so bright it is no kitchen, no sofa,

plate or building or sky or doorway you would recognise.

Gunslingers of Wane

All this time, and then it was painted over
the man's sign for his western-themed attraction,

like the end of a party, everyone back to his own thing,
no reincarnation of Dodge, some weird scenes in the mind and

the wheels stationary by late afternoon, too many of us to be
memorialised anyway, the day like scenes in a waxworks,

ring-pulls stirred at the bottom of the pond,
the edible transfer ghosts on the ice creams tasted inedible,

you are left with the feeling of things rising in early evening,
summer of indifferent vampires, bouquets afloat under wooden spars

seemed in danger, remote finding no peace in desire,
wary cowboys part of the screen's night,

twig smoke in thin air, rose gardens,
that could not be promised to anyone.

Olympic Drive

The priest had lost patience with those who would not believe.
The young men were full of rage and liked to fight.
Outside town the grain elevator was chrome and red.
Lightning at the edge of town was a blink in a mirror.
November at the pier turnstile was like they were paying for rain.
The cinema was huge and the projectionist never got old.
The park was poorly maintained and the new estate sparsely inhabited.
The roundabout didn't make sense.
Some ways are no way, some ways are split in two.
The white flowers that grew by the roadside lasted a long time despite fiery noons
Each denuded unit of labour slipping out from cleaning a hotel wall,
a thing inside his or her mind the grateful freedom which is the distorted sea,
an aimless driveway, cars asleep on shadows,
daytime bars helping reach platinum edged fences,
ryegrass straying its pearly way to the road.

Acknowledgements

Acknowledgements and thanks are due to the editors of the following magazines in which some of these poems first appeared: *Ambit*, *Cake*, *The Rialto*, *Smiths Knoll*, *Poetry Wales*.

Huge gratitude and thanks are due to my tutors: Roddy Lumsden, Ros Barber, Matthew Caley, Sasha Dugdale, Tamar Yoseloff, and Mark Waldron.

Thanks to Michael Laskey and Joanna Cutts.

Thank you to Gareth Lewis.

Thanks also to all at Eyewear: Todd Swift, Amira Ghanim and Alex Wylie.

CPSIA information can be obtained
at www.ICGtesting.com
Printed in the USA
BVHW071211160321
602610BV00003B/116

9 781913 606763